Undressing the Heart

poems by

Christine O. Adler

Finishing Line Press
Georgetown, Kentucky

Undressing the Heart

For my family

Copyright © 2021 by Christine O. Adler
ISBN 978-1-64662-389-1 First Edition
All rights reserved under International and Pan-American Copyright Conventions. No part of this book may be reproduced in any manner whatsoever without written permission from the publisher, except in the case of brief quotations embodied in critical articles and reviews.

ACKNOWLEDGMENTS

I am grateful to the editors of the publications where some of these poems first appeared:

55 Words ~ The Dance
Armenian Poetry Project ~ Breaths of Spring
Coal: A Poetry Anthology ~ Mine
Damselfly Press ~ Fool's Gold
Dr. Hurley's Snake Oil Cure ~ January, Jack
Inkwell Journal ~ Whimsy's Nest; Hummingbird
Literary Mama ~ Unearthed
The Furnace Review ~ We Live So Well
Tipton Poetry Journal ~ Middle Space
Penumbra ~ First Love

Publisher: Leah Huete de Maines
Editor: Christen Kincaid
Cover Art and Design: Alex Lindquist
Author Photo: Alex Lindquist
Cover Design: Elizabeth Maines McCleavy

Order online: www.finishinglinepress.com
also available on amazon.com

Author inquiries and mail orders:
Finishing Line Press
PO Box 1626
Georgetown, Kentucky 40324
USA

Table of Contents

First Love 1

Revelation 2

Fourth July 3

Whimsy's Nest 4

Fool's Gold 5

The Dance 7

Mine 8

Hummingbird 10

Middle Space 11

Night Shift 13

Unearthed 14

We Live So Well 16

Roots 17

Breaths of Spring 19

Cocoon 20

January, Jack 22

First Love

Crossing the vast expanse of green
at recess to ivy covered fences,
we'd stand strangely focused
for an hour on the details
of the flowers on the vine.
Pulling the pistil down
through the stem, we'd taste
the honey, a single drop drawn
from each blossom,

then race each other back

past the swings and climbing ropes
to the red brick building.
We'd laugh, panting, faces flushed
while scents of grass stains,
sweat and honeysuckle rose
up from our young skin, hot
like the sun that beat down on us
at noon in that open field.

Revelation

laughing boys
her hot, flushed cheeks: found
diary

Fourth July

Grinning, backlit
by summer's wet breath
and a tangerine sky, my sister
lies on the lawn arms and legs
starfish splayed. Hair shines
like rays from the sun of her head.

I touch the lingering burn
where the sparkler's heat met my fingers,
feel the long grass beneath my toes
cooling down in the cricket-filled gloam.
Fireflies light the night, a sea
of shifting constellations.

Whimsy's Nest

Ah, youthful ingénue, beauty
is your folly! Bare your perky breasts
like plumes and strut

your un-plucked flesh, aglow
with virgin's blush. Float
on the wind of passing years, high

above the roots of earth, light
as a sparrow's splayed wing.
Let remiges sustain your flight,

rectrices guide your back. When life's limbs
summon you down to inhabit
its branches, line your nest

with satin ribbons, pin them
with a rose's thorns as memories
of your early shine. Years

of transient whims will dull
the sculpture of your form. Smudge them
like coal beneath your weathered eyes,

watch as shadows form
in faded gray, softening you
like a grounded feather's edge.

Fool's Gold

In the chaos of our parting, you scattered
scraps of my shredded letter. Bits
of words fell to the floor, noiseless

and soft, as a lover slips into bed
beside a sleeping partner:

      sorry
          never

meant
              wish
   forgive
                 please

As the front door slammed,
they fluttered then stilled, surrounding me;
irreparable fragments of something

so recently whole, still warm in memory.
I swaddle its image, perfect, and choose
to forget that you've left me

for the kind of woman who buys herself flowers.
Spread across our bed under
the blanket of night, I slide into a fitful dream:

women move across a dance floor,
sultry, seductive, sparkling,
bright bubbles in champagne flutes. Laughter

rises as music plays, shoes shuffle and skirts
swirl while I, not knowing the steps, follow
behind, bent low and barefoot, nails unpainted.

Flakes of burnt skin fall from my feet
like black petals as I move to pick up
buttons dropped from shimmering gowns,

then hand them over, an offering:
a fistful of gold.

The Dance

Friday night, he's returned again,
grass-stained, to dance away
his loneliness. Warmed by liquor,
he whispers, "Eres una adicción"—
you are an addiction. I smile.
His money will go to my daughter
in Ecuador. Our dance will continue
next time, as we untangle ourselves
from our own joyless truths
and sway in each other's arms.

Mine

The year my dad's back
gave out, Doc Hadden read the tests
and sighed, "black lung" while mother
stood apron clad with hanky-pressed mouth,

dry eyed. Some months later came
her call, a blinking light left, found
upon my tired return from
a medical research cram.

I pulled the indexed notes, stacked
so neatly in my bag and sat,
listened to her words and flipped
through detail-crowded cards,

each a meticulous list
of disease and lethal symptoms.
I'd read their names, drop my eyes
test myself: *Scrofula: tubercular*

infection; impacts throat lymph glands.
At twenty, he'd followed his father
into the seams, ceilings dripping water. He'd lie
in mud, supine, nineteen working inches

lit only by his miner's lamp.
Yaws: chronic, relapsing infectious
illness; spirochete caused; cannot penetrate
skin. Influenza: virus; changes by mutation.

The day he told me the story of Macbeth,
the mine that blew a dark March day
and took his father's life, I knew the chain
would break. *Pneumoconiosis: also known*

as black lung disease; two forms—
simple and progressive massive fibrosis.
Miners who'd once gone below
in dark of early morning trudged

over those same entries bearing
stretchers, mangled corpses of family men.
He'd rushed the vast black cavity of Macbeth

Mine that day, stood among the town waiting.

They'd remain long, dark days, edge
the mine's mouth while rain poured down,
a town of immobile kin. The mournful
cable whine brought them to the surface

body after body

but the screams of widows rising
at each man's recognition haunt
my father still. "It's all we knew."
He shrugged his burly shoulders, pointed

his eyes downward when I made
medical school my goal instead
of coal. "It's over,"
her voice fell flatly in the room.

Cards fluttered to the floor
while I sat, eyes down understanding
that the only life I'd saved
by breaking the chain was mine.

Hummingbird

In youth you dreamt of boundless
flight, the hum of lifeblood in your veins
before love grasped your supple heart
beneath its underground

of ribs and iridescence. Your dream-song
altered, the shift of balance left you
hovering between earth and sky, hope
lodged like a bloodstone in your silken throat,

seeping ruby beauty. Threading
thorns with ribbons, you built
a nest of invisible stitches
while the shadows of life lengthened.

Lacing mercy with tears
and singular intimacies
you fashioned a proxy nirvana,
a grove of tiny salvations

while in your mind you'd fly off,
pull the threads, unravel
the stratums of sadness and joy
to craft your life anew.

Now on verdant, mirrored feathers
you dance, at once static and stirred
your wings a hazy halo
of thrumming gauze.

Swathed in a sash of vibration
and hunger, you fall headlong
into gratitude to savor
the radiant nectar of grace.

Middle Space

Early Sunday I hug my son off
to school; his cool-skinned arm
wrapped around my back, a warm,
whiskered kiss against my cheek.

After he's left I get the call:
his cousin, a passenger,
car crash last night. At high
speed, tether-free, they rolled,

were thrown. "No survivors,"
my brother breaks down.
Devastation splits me open
like a rock in summer sun.

I imagine his son, the same
young age as mine; man-boy
with parenthetical freckles around
an ever-ready grin.

Evidence of another statistic,
the roadside stone, heavy
and unyielding as grief
is already laden with flowers.

In coming months, I will drive
by the site. My heart
will clench as sunlight strikes
the stone without warning, glints

like a flare: there
then gone.

My son drives toward
his dorm, alive, still
in the world
of before, his future

stretched ahead like the bright
clear sky, awash with light. Dry-eyed
before absorbing the weight of my brush
with a mother's greatest loss

I reach slowly for the phone
to bring him home.

Night Shift

I like to think it was the poem
not yet fully-formed that woke me,
like a quickening, or a tickle in
the throat of pre-dawn darkness.

Now words fall silently
like snow inside my head,
as I lay warm, surrounded
by night sounds: baseboard tick,

furnace cough and hum, soft
snores, rising wind, roars
of occasional plows. Through years
of motherhood training, I rise

to feel across the nightstand landscape
of magazines and pens, slip
quietly into muted bathroom light,
then open my mind's faucet and pour

its contents—floating, unrelenting words—
on the white and lineless page.
By morning, this clamor
and gossamer darkness will vanish

like the dream we can't revisit.
What will remain are scribbled words
revealed like secrets in my sleep:
intangible, nocturnal guests,

begging for daylight, fleeting as thought.
Always, they come like mid-night
labor pains that push
on the edges of slumber and dawn

and even as I fight the waking
they demand, I recognize
their urgent promise of the new,
a brilliant treasure surfacing.

Unearthed
      —For Sarah

As a girl, you used to paint,
low on the walls in corners of your room,
tiny trees and flowers, undetected.

Soon boarding school called;
I was left to rearrange
the furniture, unearth your garden. We spoke

later; you laughed at the standoffs
that sparked those small
rebellions. Such colorful pictures

defiantly raised your young
psyche. Yet you haven't outgrown
the consolation of such things:

now eighteen, home from school,
I hear you slip nights
into the bathroom—the one I can't bear

to enter for the mess—and crouch
on the floor in the corner. Now
instead of producing, you peel

the paper. Flowers fall off
in little strips leaving, beneath,
bare blue walls.

I knew my body would
betray me as I aged, yet death
is not the mid-life crisis I'd expected.

But what I'm most sorry for
is what my illness does to us:
strips me by layers of physical strength,

peels you slowly in little
emotional strips until
all that's left is bare and blue.

Yet you are the unlucky one:
soon my turn will come to go.
But you will remain and be forced

to rearrange, unable to speak
with me about things you may
happen to suddenly unearth.

We Live So Well

We live so well in roles
defined by trial and error
in love, with family, each other.

Contented in selves
and routine we are thrown
a curve by illness unexpected and,
we'll come to learn, unending.

Uncertainty grips our lungs; our days
shift from living to living
through. With you unable
to sleep, eat or breathe free

of vomit, tears or pain,
the banalities of normalcy become
a fantasy we long to re-attain.
Responsibility leans

Heavy on my shoulders. Though
the children are half-grown, they know
things they shouldn't
have to so young.

I am many nouns now;
your wall to lean on, family filter
keeping upbeat, hiding details on the phone;
(it only hurts to hear them);

Mister consistency to kids and pets,
those who most need evenness.
Yet I refuse to lose hope,
even when the tests tell me

to resign myself to your
incremental fading.
Don't be afraid, Love.

I've already learned
to do so much.
Let me do that for you too.

Roots

As the late October day
slopes toward sunset, I pull up
carrots, turnips, yams from the garden
by the lake. Hairy topped and chilled,
the roots seem to yield with relief
like frozen bones freed from wintry hands.

This was our starting place,
where flat terrain seemed ripe for growth.
We turned the earth, inhaled
its musky warmth. As years crept by,
regrets collected, poisoning
the soil like salt. The lake,

calm backdrop to our missteps,
echoed only sky and evergreens.
When you left, I steadied
my reflections on its shores.
My skin and body have grown thick, protective.
Shadows of the dock and boats are dark

against the dusk. My breath mingles
with the lake's ancient sighs. They rise
in sync as evening mist, a heavy
exhalation of the day. Muted light
settles on its surface; I marvel
at the sunset, its cool, diluted sky.

Summer's growing thin; soon frost
will creep along the lawn like scars
to tinge the aging space.
We can't predict the future.
In the kitchen I will peel
piles of carrots, counting every stroke,

grounded in the moment by
the movement of the chore.
I'll undress the turnips, slip away
their skin and strip the dirt,
reveal their rawness, wet and sweet.
With orange-colored fingers

I'll wipe my tears and slice
the onions, coax them into softening
in the melting butter's warmth
as they mingle with the yams. Just a pinch
of salt before I pour the stock across my crop,
cover it like nightfall. The broth will water down

the roots' inconsistencies like passing years.
As the flavors meld, their differences
will grow elusive, fade
as interrupted growth and failings
simmer off, forgotten.

Breaths of Spring

breaths of spring
from an attic trunk
old love notes

Cocoon

Preparing for your shower, you lay
out extra towels, clothes, soap
for the 'others' who might join you.
Some days, they are soldiers.

Most nights, you wake and want
to go home, to San Antone where
you lived with your mom and sister
in nineteen fifty. They're both long gone.

When I find you moving furniture
around the den again, looking for
your lost, unnamable treasure and retreat,
you crossly accuse me of theft.

You whisper to the room "*that girl
does not like me.*" I hide
the knives and scissors, bury
them deep under linens.

As I move, I listen to the weatherman
tell me what to count on. Things I know for sure:
the heat in Oklahoma is sickening the cows;
wildfires threaten relentlessly.

Standing at the sink, I rinse a bowl
of berries under running water;
its sound drowns out your threats.
When disease seizes you

in its periodic grip and steals
our past from me, I take comfort
in believing there's a secret
behind what torments you.

Here in the kitchen, the walls are webs
woven from old conversations. Words
from mundane moments, inside jokes
and pillow talks perch like dew drops

on the silk. Light glimmers through them,
turns the words to diamonds.
I want to wrap you in
this diamond-studded silk:

spin a cocoon strong and binding,
one from which you'll never emerge,
never become someone
I no longer know.

January, Jack
     —For Lorna

On your birthday I step out
before sunrise to view the lake, the same
as every morning since our final
Saturday. I succumb

to ritual as you did to pain, let it become
my keel, the core from which I measure
just what color life is now. In the bluing
air, reflected trees stand top sides down,

knobby trunks lined, bases-up, like brushes
hung to dry. On the quiet water surface,
its black plate flushed
with rose and lavender beneath

the sprawling dawn, they paint a picture limned
in memories and fog. I've passed
a summer of blown dandelions
and dead cicada shells; in autumn, leaves

fell to earth like broken hopes. Kindly-worded
watercolor cards stopped coming
about the time the dock's ladder
began to gather rungs of snow. Today

I hear you through the grief: a veil
of gray geese rises toward the sky. Backlit
they scatter like ashes, their low,
recurring call persists

Get on, get on.

Its meaning seeps in by degrees
like the dawn, a solid promise kept
that day will come again. Finally it arrives,
a surprise—at once sudden and complete—

to bear its beating heart,
a golden hub of sun.

Christine Orchanian Adler is a writer and editor whose poetry has appeared in *Coal: A Poetry Anthology, Inkwell, Penumbra, Tipton Poetry Journal,* and online at *Bird and Moon, Damselfly Press, The Furnace Review, Literary Mama* and elsewhere. Her chapbook, *Undressing the Heart,* won an honorable mention in the Palettes & Quills 3rd Biennial Chapbook Contest. She served as a judge in the Greenburgh Arts & Culture Committee's 35th Poetry Contest; The Harvey School's annual Michael Lopes Poetry Recitation Contest, and as Editor and Managing Editor of *Inkwell*. Her articles, essays and book reviews have appeared in various publications throughout the Northeastern United States and Canada. She blogs at www.christineoadler.com and is currently at work on a novel. She lives in New York with her husband and sons. Twitter: @ChristineAdler Instagram: animalfeeder

www.ingramcontent.com/pod-product-compliance
Lightning Source LLC
LaVergne TN
LVHW041523070426
835507LV00012B/1771

9 781646 623891